People from Jericho

**The stories of
famous Bible characters
by
Colin Morison**

Their lives and how God used them

Design
Clifton Collier Advertising Limited
6 Rubislaw Place, Aberdeen AB1 1XN

Artwork and Illustrations
Art Works Limited
6 Rubislaw Place, Aberdeen AB1 1XN

Photographs courtesy of
Bible Scene Slide Tours
26 Home Close, Sharnbrook,
Bedford MK44 1PQ

Published in Great Britain by
Christian Focus Publications Limited
Geanies House, Fearn, Tain,
Ross-shire IV20 1TW, Scotland

© 1985 Christian Focus Publications Ltd.
ISBN 0 906731 364

Contents

On knocking down walls

ave you ever tried to knock down a wall? I am sure that if you have you will realise what a big job it is. Without the right tools we would be quite unable to do the job properly.

If we were to tackle the walls of a city we would say that not only would we need the right tools but we would also need a lot of people working very hard to knock them down. However if we turn in our Bibles to the book of Hebrews, chapter 11, verse 30, we are told that by **faith** the walls of Jericho fell down.

There had been a walled city called Jericho on that site for many years before our story begins. Jericho had stood up to many invasions and had been destroyed by invading armies and then rebuilt. Always people returned to Jericho to take refuge behind its secure walls. But if it is by faith that the walls of Jericho came tumbling down then this means that faith is stronger than walls or cities or anything else made by man.

We are going to learn about the faith of people like Elisha who purified the water of Jericho, of blind Bartimaeus who received his sight and of Zacchaeus who learned to trust in Jesus rather than in money. From these people we will see how strong and important faith is and how it could knock down walls.

Spying out the land

Jericho is probably most famous because of its walls. Or perhaps it would be more correct to say Jericho is famous because of what God, through the armies of Israel, did to these walls. So let us look more closely at what happened.

Jericho was an important town in the land of Canaan when the Israelites, under Joshua, attacked and invaded it. It was close to the River Jordan, very close to the borders of the land of Canaan. The invading Israelites would naturally have to do something about Jericho.

What would be one of the first things a good leader would do? Joshua, as a general invading a foreign land clearly had to spy out the land to see what were the most difficult parts of it to conquer. Then he could make his plans to defeat his enemies.

Joshua was careful although he had every reason to be confident of his victory. In fact God had spoken very personally to Joshua. God had said to him, 'In three days you will cross the Jordan and go on to take over the land which I have promised to you.' Although Joshua had God's definite promise that the land was theirs to possess, yet he wanted to check out the land, as any good general would.

So he sent in two spies and told them, 'Look over the land, especially the town of Jericho.'

The two spies set off on their dangerous mission. Secretly they entered the town of Jericho and there they met a lady called Rahab whose house formed part of the wall of Jericho. From Rahab they found out that although Jericho was a strong city with an army and big walls for its defence, the king and all the people who lived there were afraid of the Israelites. They had heard of the powerful way in which God had helped the Israelites, how He had dried up the Red Sea, and how He had brought them through the desert.

The things that God does for His people are often noticed more by others than by those for whom they are done. The Israelites had complained so many times of the hardships which they had had to suffer, yet their enemies were able to see what God had done for them. It is often true of us that we grumble about the problems of life — when others can see what marvellous things He is doing in our lives.

The two spies must have been very interested to hear how afraid of God the people of Jericho were and of what might happen to them. The men must surely have been eager to get back to Joshua to tell him the position in Jericho.

But they had been seen entering the city and this news had been reported to the king. Immediately he sent his messengers to Rahab telling her to bring out the spies. Rahab, however, hid the men on the roof of her house and when the messengers came she said, 'The men left the city in the evening, so I don't know where they have gone.' So the messengers went after the spies. But why had Rahab helped these two men? Rahab hid the spies so that she could talk to them and make plans to save herself and her family.

RAHAB'S AGREEMENT WITH THE ISRAELITE SPIES

The men made an agreement with Rahab that if she hid them and did not tell about their visit and their spying activities they would make sure that Rahab and her family were saved at the time of attack on the city. They told Rahab that she must be sure to put a scarlet cord in her window so that she could be indentified and saved from death.

Rahab then told them that it would be safe for them to go and hide in the hills beyond Jericho for three days until all the pursuers had returned to the city. Then the men could go back to their own army unharmed.

When the spies left Jericho they promised Rahab that they would make sure that her life and those of her family would be spared, and

that their own lives would be
forfeit if they didn't keep to this
promise.

After spending a few days
hiding in the hills the spies made
their way back to the other side of
the Jordan to make their report to
Joshua. Joshua, as a good
commander, now had the
information he wanted — and
could make preparations for
crossing into the land of Canaan.

CROSSING THE JORDAN

Of course every commander likes to know that he has the approval of the superiors who are behind him. Joshua's supreme commander was God, and he was trusting that God would show him the way ahead. As Joshua trusted in God, God gave him another demonstration of His power. He told Joshua, 'Tell the priests to take the ark of the covenant and stand in the waters of the River Jordan.' When they had done this God made the waters stop flowing so that the Israelites were able to walk across the river quite dry — and this was at a time when the River Jordan was in flood!

After this the Israelites stopped to set up an altar to praise and thank God for his help. It is important that we do this as well. Often when we get good things from God we forget that we should stop and thank God for what He has done for us. It does not matter how busy we are, or how important our business is, we should thank God for His goodness to us. After all, if the Israelites could stop in the middle of the invasion of a hostile land surely we can see that it is very important.

So at a place called Gilgal the Israelite nation rested and prepared themselves for the battles ahead.

It may seem that a great deal of preparation had to be done before attacking Jericho — especially as God had promised Joshua that they would win and the spies had found out that everyone was scared of them.

But as we shall see later, the preparation was important for two reasons. One was to prepare the Israelites to believe that it was God who was doing the work, and not themselves. The other reason was to show the people of Canaan the power of the Israelites' God and the blessings that would come to those who put their trust not in their own cleverness but in God.

The fall of Jericho

Before any major battle, generals and commanding officers meet together to prepare a plan of campaign, so that they know the way they want the battle to go. Often they have secret meetings to stop the enemy from finding out their plans. Joshua was no exception.

On the day before the siege of Jericho began, Joshua slipped out of the camp to look at the city and see what its defences were like.

Suddenly he noticed a man approaching him — a man with a drawn sword in his hand. Joshua challenged the man, 'Are you with us or with our enemy?' The man replied, 'I am captain of God's army.'

JOSHUA RECEIVES HIS INSTRUCTIONS

Hearing this Joshua realised that God had sent an angel to direct him and to lead the attack

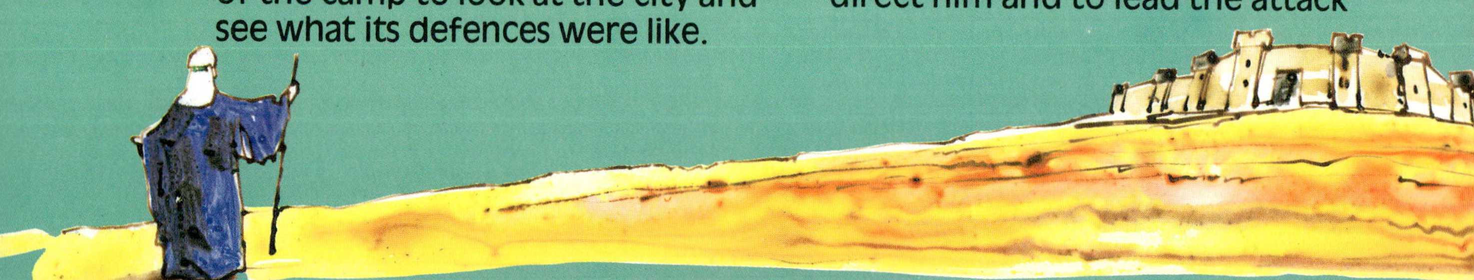

on Jericho. He fell down on his knees and worshipped the captain of the armies of God, and asked for his advice.

If we had been there we would have been surprised by the tactics that were given to Joshua. We might expect to hear of swords and spears, and of ladders to scale the walls. We might expect to hear of a battering ram to knock down the gates. What Joshua was told, however, was that his army was to walk round the city!

Once a day, for six days, the armies of Israel were to walk round the city of Jericho. They were to be led by the priests and were to walk round in silence. We find it difficult to keep silent for six minutes, but all these people were to keep silent and make no noise for six days!

On the seventh day the priests would blow the ramshorns which they carried, the people would all give a great shout and the walls of Jericho would fall flat.

Joshua called the priests together and passed on to them the instructions he had been given. They must lead the people of Israel round the walls of Jericho for the next six days, and then on the seventh day they would see the walls tumble flat and the city would be theirs.

Down in Jericho the gates were

tightly shut, no one came in or went out, night or day, as the Israelites drew near. Great fear and tension were felt in the city as they waited for something to happen. They knew of the power of the God who led these Israelites and they were afraid of the dreadful things that might happen to them.

Imagine then their surprise at what did happen. Instead of charging up to the city with drawn swords and battering rams, the Israelite army began to march slowly and silently round the walls of Jericho. For six long days they marched round, without so much as a shout. Inside Jericho the terrified people waited and waited, wondering what would happen.

THE WALLS OF JERICHO FALL

Then on the seventh day the priests stopped and blew their horns. Joshua shouted to the people. 'Shout out, because God has given us the city.' The people all shouted out and with a great roar the walls of Jericho began to fall in, and crumble. The ground shook as those mighty rocks and stones came crashing to the ground.

Inside the city the people fled in panic to their homes as the Israelite army surged in to the city which God had given them. Confusion reigned everywhere as men died and homes were destroyed.

Somewhere in the middle of it all were Rahab and her family — perhaps praying that God would keep her safe and that the spies would remember their promise. Joshua the wise commander had remembered the commitment that they had made. He directed the two men to go into the city, to

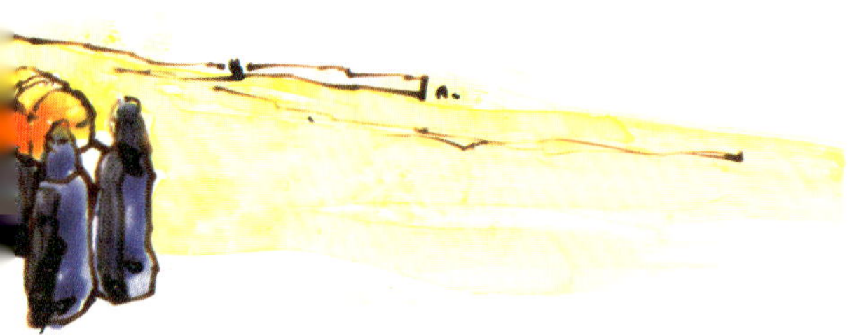

find Rahab and her family and to bring them safely to the camp outside the city walls.

The young men went off quickly to find their friend and helper. They found her as she had promised — in her house with all her family, with the scarlet cord tied in the window, and very quickly they took her and her family out of Jericho into the Israelite camp and to safety.

It was as well that they had done this because Joshua had ordered that the city of Jericho and all of its belongings and inhabitants should be destroyed by fire.

It may seem strange or even cruel to us that the Israelites should destroy the city and kill all its inhabitants.

The reason for doing this was that the people of Jericho had disobeyed God, and God knew that they were wicked. He wished them to be destroyed because the sin that they committed had to be destroyed so that the Israelite people would not become affected by this sin.

It may seem to us to be very hard on all the people of Jericho — but we must remember that the same God who allowed the deaths of the people at the flood in Noah's day and now in Jericho, also sent His only Son to die for us.

Another thing that is clear is that it was God who knocked down the walls of Jericho. The people of Israel did not blow up the walls, or climb them with rope ladders. What they had to do was to obey God and trust that if they did as He said then the battle would be won for them.

All that God asked was obedience and trust. He did not require great skill or fighting ability, or even great brain power. All He required was that they trust and obey Him.

Yet as we shall see even that was too much for the Israelites — for one of the army of Israel was tempted to disobey and so he brought disaster on his fellow countrymen.

Achan's sin

When God told Joshua how to conquer Jericho, He also said to Joshua that the goods and people were all to be destroyed but the gold, silver and brass were all to be given to God.

However when the Israelites went into Jericho they must have seen many beautiful and attractive things. Many of them were probably tempted to take something back with them, perhaps thinking that out of all the things in Jericho no one would notice one small thing. Most of the Israelites resisted this temptation but one of them, a man called Achan, took some goods back to his tent in the camp-site.

The effects of this sin were not immediately noticed. Achan most likely thought that his theft was a secret, known only to himself. He was wrong, because God knew and was angry.

We may think that the things we do are secret — and we may think like Achan that, out of so much, a small sin like ours will not be noticed and will do no harm to anyone. But God knows, and it hurts God when we disobey Him. It does not matter how small the thing we do, if it is against God's will then we are hurting Him, and it may lead to greater hurt and pain not only to ourselves but to others.

Achan found this out very quickly. Shortly after the destruction of Jericho, Joshua announced that they would spy out Ai — a city not far away. The spies reported back and said that Ai was a smaller city, that two or three thousand men could defeat it without difficulty. So Joshua sent the men forward to Ai — but instead of an easy victory the Israelites were defeated losing thirty-six of their men.

Joshua was amazed. What could have happened? He could have held an enquiry into the reasons for defeat, but instead he did the right thing. He asked God what was wrong. Often we get into difficulties and the first thing we do is try to work out what we did wrong. The most important thing we should do is to ask God why we have gone wrong. He is more able than anyone in the world to direct us, and will always tell us how to put things right if we ask Him.

When Joshua asked what had gone wrong, God told him that they had lost because of disobedience, because someone from the Israelite army had stolen things from the city of Jericho.

Joshua then gathered all the Israelite people together and, guided by God, he found out who was the guilty man. When Achan was pointed out as the man guilty of disobedience and theft, he admitted his wrongdoing, and told everyone present that he had taken a robe, some silver and some gold, and hid it in the ground underneath his tent. Achan, of course, had to be punished. God commanded that he and all his family should be killed as punishment for what he had done.

So Achan's sin was punished. We can see then that his seemingly little sin affected many people. It is like that, too, when we sin. We hurt and affect many others when we do wrong. But worst of all we hurt God when we sin and we must

remember that above all else.

The town rebuilt

When Joshua saw Jericho destroyed, he placed a curse on it. He said that whoever tried to rebuild Jericho would lose his oldest and youngest sons.

Many years after the time of Joshua a man called Hiel, from Bethel, rebuilt Jericho. We do not know why he rebuilt Jericho. He lived during the time of Ahab who was one of the most wicked kings Israel had ever had. Hiel probably rebuilt Jericho with Ahab's permission or even at the request of Ahab — because Jericho had been an important town fairly near the borders of Israel and not

very far from Jerusalem.

JOSHUA'S WORDS COME TRUE

During the preparations — as
the foundations for the new
Jericho were being laid — Hiel's
oldest son, Abiram, died. Then
when work had progressed and
the gates of the new city were set
up, the youngest of Hiel's sons,
Segub, also died. So the words of
Joshua came true.

We don't know how the people
who were working on the building
of the city felt about all this, but
surely it would be true to say that
Hiel did not believe the words of
Joshua, or he would not have done
the work. We are often like that.
We will sometimes not believe that
God will punish us, or refuse to
believe that God carries out all His
promises — but we must realise
that God always does exactly as He
says. Perhaps some of the people
of Jericho believed in God when
they saw Joshua's word come true.
We do not know for certain about
these things but what we can say is
that God's word is always true.

A man who did believe that
God's words were true was Elijah.
Elijah was a prophet who lived
during the time of king Ahab. Elijah
spoke out very strongly against
some of the things that Ahab was
doing. When the time came for

Elijah to die he went with his successor Elisha to the River Jordan, as God directed him. As they went towards Jordan they passed Jericho. At that time Jericho must have been quite an important religious centre because there were a considerable number of prophets living there. As Elijah and Elisha came towards Jericho the prophets came out from the city to welcome them and to tell Elisha that God would soon be taking his master away. Fifty of the prophets from Jericho came out of the city to watch what would happen.

Elijah and Elisha crossed the River Jordan. On the far side of the river Elijah was taken away by God to Heaven. So Elisha returned to the other side and prepared to carry on God's work.

ELISHA HEALS THE BAD WATER OF JERICHO

While he was staying in Jericho, the men of the city came to Elisha and told him that although the city was in a good location the water was bad and this made the land poor and unproductive. Elisha asked for some salt, to throw into the spring which gave water to the city. When he had thrown the salt into the spring, Elisha turned to the men and told them that God had purified the water.

It seems strange to us that salt should be used to purify water. If we put salt in our fresh drinking water it becomes unpleasant, or if we water out plants with salty water they will die. Yet here was Elisha telling the people of Jericho that salt would cure their bad water!

We cannot say exactly why the salt healed the bad water, but we can be sure that God knew why the water was bad because it was part of His creation and He knew the best way to cure the things which were wrong with it. Perhaps salt was used so that people would know that God had made their

water pure. We do not know everything about ourselves or about the world that we are in, but we can believe that God does know everything, and when He comands we must obey. As David says in the Psalms, 'Your word is a lamp to my feet and a light for my path.'

Jesus and Jericho

Jesus Christ travelled all over the countryside preaching to people, telling them of their need of a Saviour and of their need to believe in God and to do what God wanted.

On his travels Jesus came to Jericho. Once he told the story that is known to us as the parable of the Good Samaritan. The story was about a man travelling on the lonely and dangerous road between Jerusalem and Jericho. Now Jesus himself was there. Jericho would not have been anything at all like the place to which Joshua came when the

Israelites invaded Canaan. In many ways, though, the people who lived in Jericho were no different from those who had lived there when the walls collapsed. There were some people, many people in fact, who did not believe in God's words, who did not follow God's teaching. There were only a few like Rahab who believed in God and believed that Jesus was the Son of God.

JESUS HEALS BLIND BARTIMAEUS

One man who came to believe in Jesus was Bartimaeus. Bartimaeus lived in Jericho. He was a blind man, and in those days blind men were not able to work, they could not live in nice homes, or be looked after by others. In order to survive blind people had to sit at the side of the roads leading into the cities, for hour after hour, day after day, begging for money or food.

Bartimaeus would sit like this for hours and hours just holding out his bowl and asking people to give him something as they passed.

Day after day it would be just the same; hot, dry, dusty — perhaps he was sometimes fearful that someone might come and steal out of his bowl instead of putting something in.

This day, however, was different. There was something different about the feet that went past his spot. For one thing there were far more of them than usual and for another the way that they hurried past instead of stopping to speak told him that they were excited about something. He asked those nearest to him what was happening. Somebody told him, 'Jesus of Nazareth is passing by on his way into Jericho.'

At this the blind man began to shout, perhaps in the hope that someone would take notice of him and lead him to Jesus. He shouted out, 'Jesus, Son of David, have mercy on me.'

Some of those round about him were embarrassed by all the noise. They felt that here was a blind beggar bringing shame on the whole town of Jericho by his noisy and rowdy behaviour. They quickly told him to be quiet. But Bartimaeus had no intention of being quiet. Deep down he knew that this might be his last chance of getting back his sight. Jesus, the worker of miracles, was in town and he must attract his attention. He shouted out even louder, 'Son of David, have mercy on me.'

Jesus heard the cry, as he had heard so many before, and he stopped. 'Bring that man to me', he said.

When Bartimaeus was brought to him Jesus said, 'What is it that you want me to do?' Bartimaeus replied, 'Lord, I want to be able to see.'

So Jesus replied to him, 'Your sight is restored to you. Your faith in me has saved you from blindness.'

Immediately Bartimaeus was able to see, and of course he was overjoyed! He followed Jesus as he went through the town, praising God and telling everyone that he met about what had happened.

When Jesus had said to Bartimaeus that his faith had saved him from blindness he didn't mean just that Bartimaeus could see with his eyes. Jesus also meant that Bartimaeus had faith which saved him from what God calls spiritual blindness. This means that if we do not have faith then we cannot see God because the wrong things we do hide God from us. If, like Bartimaeus, we have faith in Jesus then the wrong deeds are taken away by Jesus and then we can see God.

ZACCHAEUS THE TAX-COLLECTOR

Another person in Jericho at this time who wanted to see Jesus was a little fellow called Zacchaeus. Zacchaeus was a tax-collector. This meant that he collected money from the people of Jericho to give to the Romans who ruled Palestine. For this reason Zacchaeus was not very popular with the citizens of Jericho. He also made himself more unpopular by collecting more money than he needed to. Some of this he kept for himself and so became very rich. However because he was rich through cheating the people of Jericho he was disliked by many of them — something which made him unhappy.

So Zacchaeus decided to see this man Jesus. He had heard all about the miracles of Jesus, and perhaps he thought that Jesus would be able to work a miracle and make all the people of Jericho friendly towards Zacchaeus. Now that is exactly what Jesus did but in a way that Zacchaeus could hardly have expected.

Zacchaeus left his house to go down to the main street to see if he could see Jesus. Being a very small man, though, he could not see over the heads of the crowd — so he decided to go and find a tree to climb from where he would get a better view. He ran on ahead of the crowd. Just by the roadside he spotted a sycamore tree, not too difficult to climb and with good broad branches so that he could rest comfortably and wait for this extraordinary man Jesus to arrive.

'And he ran before, and climbed into
a sycamore tree to see him …'
Luke, Chapter 19, verse 4

Zacchaeus hoped that Jesus would just walk past and he would be able to get a good look at him to see what kind of man Jesus was.

What a surprise it must have been for him to see Jesus stopping not far away from the tree, and moving forward to look into the centre of it. How embarrassed he must have been — one of the richest men in the city, one of its most important citizens — caught in a tree with a huge crowd gathered round looking at him.

What would he do? He could not get away without looking foolish. He would have to wait for the crowd to depart before he could slip down and go home quietly.

But then Jesus spoke to him. 'Zacchaeus, hurry up and come down from that tree. I want to stay in your house tonight.'

Well, we can imagine that Zacchaeus was as pleased as could be. Here was the famous Jesus of Nazareth wanting to stay in his house. That would make up for all the unpopularity and the undignified climb down from the tree! In front of all the people of Jericho, Jesus had actually asked to stay in his house.

So together Zacchaeus and Jesus went back to the house. No doubt they talked a lot together, and as they talked Zacchaeus discovered that his guest was a demanding one. It was not enough just to welcome Jesus into his home. Zacchaeus also would have to make amends for all his cheating and stealing; to give back what he had taken and return to those that he had tricked. When Jesus saw that Zacchaeus was not only happy to have him as a guest but was also willing to give up his riches to the poor, he was glad and said that salvation had come to that house.

We see that Jesus made demands on Zacchaeus after he was taken in to the house. This is true of us also. When Jesus asks to come into our lives and we say yes to him he will make demands upon our lives. He will ask that we throw out the bad things, the wrong thoughts and that we will be like Zacchaeus, willing to do what pleases Jesus.

What a day it had been for Jericho. First of all the beggar Bartimaeus had been healed of blindness and was running round like a young child with a new present. Then the richest and possibly the meanest man in Jericho had begun to give away his possessions to those who needed them. Jesus had walked in through the gates of Jericho and had turned the place upside down. Everyone must have been talking about this amazing man.

If we accept Jesus then let us pray that when others see the change in our lives they will talk about this amazing man Jesus, the Son of God, who turned not only Jericho but the whole world upside down.

Tel-Es-Sultan — A modern name for an ancient city

Tel-Es-Sultan is the modern name for the city we know as Jericho. By today's standards it is no longer a city. In 1967 the population was only about 7000 people. But due to the war between Israel and the Arab countries some of the people moved away so Jericho is now quite a small place. Its real importance lies in its past.

In fact, Jericho today is about two and a half miles from the city whose walls were knocked down by God's power to make way for the invading army of Israel. The ruins of the old city are still there and archaeologists search amongst them to try to discover how people of long ago lived.

If we were to drive down from Jerusalem to Jericho we would do so on a modern road, unlike the travellers of old who had a long and uncomfortable journey. We would be coming from a city over 3000 feet up in the hills of Judea to a place in the desert 800 feet below sea-level. We would also see many green plants, palm trees, and grass growing in this unlikely part in the desert. These plants grow because in the middle of Jericho there is a stream called the 'Spring of Elisha'. This is the same spring of water which was made clean by the prophet thousands of years ago. So the way in which God works can be seen affecting how people live today. God is the same God who helped those who trusted in Him long ago and He still wants us to believe in Him and follow His laws.

As a result of Jericho's position

Ruins of Herod's winter palace

below sea-level and its very good water supply people visit the town on holiday. Perhaps we might think that only in modern times would this happen but even in Bible times Jericho was really a holiday resort for the kings and governors of Israel. Herod the Great, who ruled over Israel when Jesus was born, had a winter palace built for himself near Jericho. The warmer, drier winters of Jericho were far more healthy than those of Jerusalem.

Many scholars believe that Jericho is one of the oldest cities in the world. Often cities come into being because of their position. With its warm, dry climate and a good water supply Jericho was able to support all the people who lived there so it is quite likely that it has been in existence for a long time.

We do not know just how old it is but the God who created the stones and earth which made up the walls of Jericho has remained the same throughout all the changes that have taken place in the life of the city. He has watched its rise and its fall. More importantly He has watched over the lives of the people who have lived there over perhaps thousands of years.

That same God is watching over us today; and the power that

made the water in the spring of
Elisha clean, and brought the walls
of Jericho tumbling down, can be
felt in our lives today if we are
willing to trust in Him.

Joshua, Elisha, Zacchaeus, and
many others have put their trust in
God and He has helped them. If we
do as they have done we too will
find that God will help us
throughout our whole lives.